Designed by Flowerpot Press
www.FlowerpotPress.com
CHC-0909-0607
ISBN: 978-1-4867-2970-8
Made in China/Fabriqué en Chine

HOW DO YOU TURN DATA INTO DRAWINGS?

A STATISTICS BOOK ABOUT GRAPHS AND DATA

KEY

Cat

Dog

Fish

written by
clayton tobias grider
illustrated by
srimalie bassani

The average American eats almost 1,996 pounds of food per year!

The average American eats nearly 20 pounds of ice cream per year.

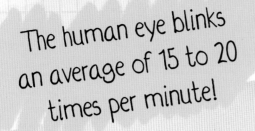

The human eye blinks an average of 15 to 20 times per minute!

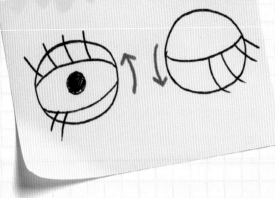

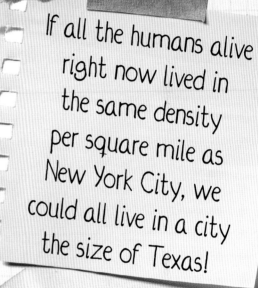

If all the humans alive right now lived in the same density per square mile as New York City, we could all live in a city the size of Texas!

You see statistics every day, whether it's in advertisements, the news, or video games. Even your favorite sports team uses statistics to help them figure out what they are doing well and what they need to work on! It is important to understand statistics for you to figure out which statistics are good statistics. That is why the subject of statistics is not just about using numbers and formulas; it is also about being able to correctly interpret them.

A future statistician like yourself will use statistics and its tools to help you be more informed about many things that affect our daily lives and even help you make predictions!

DESCRIPTIVE

1. Works with a smaller data set
2. Process is simpler
3. Results obtained represent the entire data set
4. Possible chance of error is not as high

How do you tell the difference between the two kinds of statistics? Do you flip a coin and call it in the air?

No, you don't have to choose. You use the two kinds of statistics for different reasons.

Descriptive statistics are numbers or figures that describe something. This includes collecting, organizing, summarizing, and presenting data. What is data? Data consists of individual facts or information that is usually represented by numbers. Some good examples of data are the number of people that get on the train on a particular day, the number of birds on a telephone wire, or the average number of chips in a chip bag.

So three of these bags had 250 chips each?

Yes, please don't make me eat any more chips...

INFERENTIAL

1. Works with a large data set
2. Process is more complex as you have to decide on the best sampling techniques
3. Results obtained represent a portion of the population but can be used to deduce information about the entire population with some amount of uncertainty
4. Possible chance of error is higher

As for inferential statistics, these are statistics that you use to make predictions and inferences (which are fancy words for guesses). As a statistician, you would take the data that is collected from a small group and use it to make guesses about a much larger group called the population.

If you asked your class (the small group) what each person's favorite sport is and most of them said soccer, you can take that data and infer that the majority of students at your school (the population) like soccer the most. You just did inferential statistics!

DESCRIPTIVE STATISTICS

To highlight the differences between the two types of statistics, let's try it out!

If you asked your family what their favorite color is, then you could make a table like the one below. What kind of statistics would that data represent?

Descriptive statistics! You collected the descriptive data (the colors your family members like the best) and then organized it into a table.

2 out of 4 family members said blue is their favorite color!

Individual	Favorite Color
Mom	Blue
Dad	Green
Sister	Blue
Grandpa	Orange

Say you have an assumption (something you think is right). You assume that individuals who wear blue shirts tend to have higher test scores in math than individuals who wear red shirts. You collect a sample of data that includes the students in your math class and conduct a test to find out if your assumption is correct. What kind of statistics is this?

Hypothesis testing will help us!

Now we can take our test!

Inferential statistics! After obtaining the data, you ran a test to see if your assumption was correct. This kind of testing is called hypothesis testing and is one of many tools in inferential statistics. The benefit of inferential statistics is that you do not have to have all the data to make a conclusion. Imagine trying to obtain and organize all the test scores of children in the world. That would take forever! Statistics allows us to take a smaller portion of the population to draw accurate conclusions.

Hypothesis

DATA COLLECTION

How do you collect data? Do you make your dog fetch it from your neighbors?

Dogs like fetching balls not data! This would also lead to bad information, and you would not be able to accurately show any data that you collected.

Collecting good data is important because you cannot always have the whole data set. Think about the example with the math test scores. Imagine trying to get all the test scores of all the children in math classes in the whole world. It would be hard to get all the scores even just from your school. With that said, there are many ways to collect data, and each way has its own advantages and disadvantages.

One of the main ways to get data is by collecting it through random sampling. This means that the individuals you collect data from have no pattern and are not related. The simplest form of random sampling is exactly that: the simple random sample. This process calls for choosing individuals randomly from the whole population.

Random sampling is the way to go!

COLLECTING DATA

Question: Favorite animal?

Assign a number to all students.

Choose 50 random students to collect data from.

Answers

Say you wanted to know what animal the students at your school like best. It would be hard to ask every single student, so instead you assign every student a number and randomly draw 50 numbers from a hat. Now you can get 50 random answers from 50 random students and determine what animal the students in your school like best. You have collected random data!

An example of non-random sampling is voluntary sampling. This method relies on asking volunteers to provide data. Voluntary samplings tend to be easier, cheaper, and quicker than random samplings. The down side of this method is that it tends to be filled with bias, and statisticians don't like bias! That is why they like to use random sampling.

As you can see in the chart below, there are a few types of random sampling. These kinds of samplings tend to look at the whole population.

The purpose of these different types of data collection methods is to make sure there is not a lot of bias in your sample!

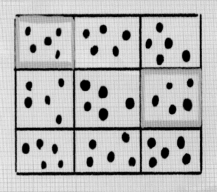

TYPES OF RANDOM SAMPLING

RANDOM SAMPLE	STRATIFIED RANDOM SAMPLE	CLUSTERED RANDOM SAMPLE
Each sample has an equal chance of being chosen from the larger population.	The larger population is divided into groups called strata before samples are selected.	The larger population is already divided into natural groups and samples are selected from those groups.

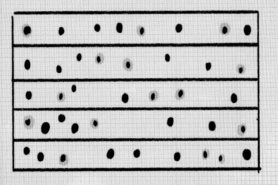

DATA BIAS

How can you identify and reduce bias in a sample? Do you buy a magnifying glass and look at the data closely to find all the bias?

No! You don't need a magnifying glass to find the bias.

Bias is the statistician's tendency to underestimate or overestimate things when analyzing and interpreting data. Your survey results may be different from the actual results because of it. That is why statisticians mostly use random sampling. They do it, not because it is fun (even though stats is fun!), but because they are attempting to reduce any chance of there being bias in their data. For your results to be right, you have to reduce your biases!

How do I get the best results?

Be sure to reduce your biases!

VOLUNTARY RESPONSE BIAS

What's your favorite cupcake?

Carrot Cake Cupcakes Fan Club

There are many types of biases that exist. For example, if you were going to collect a voluntary sample to determine your school's favorite cupcake flavor, instead of going around to your classmates and asking them, you decide to make a poster and ask for volunteers.

But there is one problem! The only people who volunteer to answer your question all belong to an after-school club called the Carrot Cake Cupcakes Fan Club. Carrot cake cupcakes seem to be the result of your survey, but the only reason for that is because the people who volunteered to answer your question felt so strongly. This kind of bias is called voluntary response bias.

Recall bias is a bias that comes from the ability of the individual to remember things in the past. Asking your parents what their favorite color was when they were in elementary school might not be easy for them. This misremembering can lead to bias in your data.

RECALL BIAS

One of the most important and spookiest types of bias to keep in mind is omitted variable bias. This happens when statisticians miss something very important in their research. Say you collected a random sample and found that your school's favorite animal was a panda and then decided to do the same survey at another school. But based on the random sampling at your school, you guess that the other school's favorite animal will also be a panda. After completing the survey, their favorite animal is actually an alligator. What could you have missed? Well, you missed the fact that your school's mascot is the Punctual Panda and the other school's mascot is the Angry Alligator. You omitted that important variable, and it may have skewed your results!

BAR GRAPH

Y-AXIS

X-AXIS

300

200

100

280

115

55

Eagle Penguin Robin

450 Total Responses

How do you graph data? Do you hire a robotic bird to draw your favorite number?

No, but that would be a very cool doodle and a very cool bird!

Graphs are a way to visually represent data. They come in all sorts of shapes and sizes! One of the most popular ways to graph data is the bar graph. It's called that because you use bars to represent the data.

So how does a bar graph work? Take a look at the graph on the left side of the page. First, let's talk about the lines. Those lines are called axes. The x-axis is at the bottom and goes from left to right. This is where you would put what you are measuring (in this case, different species of birds). As for the y-axis, it goes up and down. The numbers on the y-axis represent the number of the things being measured.

Bar graphs are neat because they make it easy to see the responses at a quick glance. In this example, penguins received 280 responses, so the blue bar (representing penguins) would go up to 280. The blue bar is much bigger than the red and yellow bars, so it means penguins got the most votes.

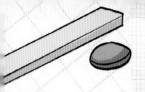

A bar graph is not the only way to visualize data. Another popular way to do it is with a pie chart. (Pie charts are the best because pie is the best food!)

In the bird data case, there were 280 responses for penguins out of 450. Pie charts represent data as percents, so 280 people out of 450 is about 62%. (To figure this out simply divide 280 by 450 and shift the decimal point to the left twice!) Eagles received 115 responses out of 450, so that would be about 26% of the pie. Robins received only 55 responses out of 450, which is about 12%. If you take those percentages and add them to the pie chart, it would look a lot like the chart on the left side of the page!

Pie charts are also very easy to read. The greatest number of responses covers the majority of the pie.

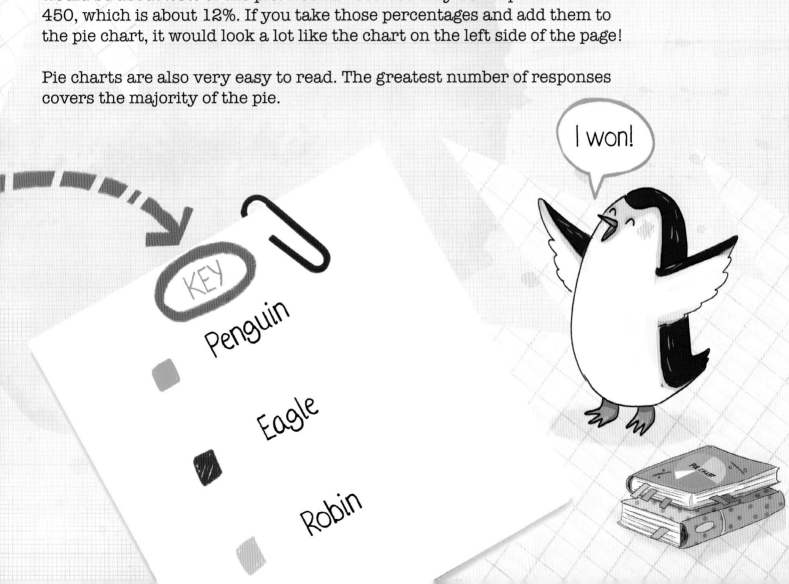

I won!

KEY

Penguin

Eagle

Robin

How can graphs be wrong and how do you know a good graph from a bad graph? Will a good graph offer you a cookie?

No, graphs won't offer you cookies, but there are a few things you will have to look out for that will tell you if the graph is misrepresenting the data.

One of the biggest giveaways are the axes. Remember the x-axis and the y-axis? They can sometimes give the numbers they are representing a biased view.

Look at the graph. The distance between 200 and 300 is MUCH larger than between 100 and 200. This graph gives the impression that the 300 is much larger than the other data points. But that is not the case. The numbers on the y-axis need to be evenly spaced in order to represent the data accurately.

It's also a good idea to keep your bars the same size too.

EXAMPLES OF INCORRECT GRAPHS

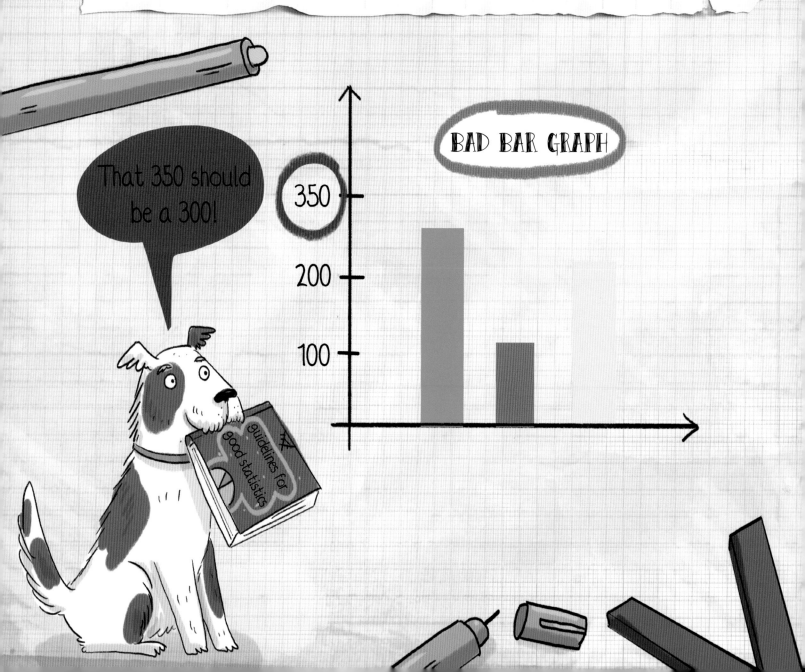

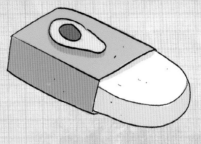

Making sure the numbers on the y-axis are consistent is also important! Look at the graph on the left side of the page.

The numbers on the y-axis are 100, 200, and 350. The graph was counting by 100, so 300 should be next. The 350 makes the data in between 200 and 350 look closer to the numbers between 100 and 200 than they actually are.

As for pie charts, make sure the total of all your data adds up to 100%. They say you should always give 110%, but not in pie charts! All the numbers must add up to 100.

The numbers on this pie chart don't add up to 100%!

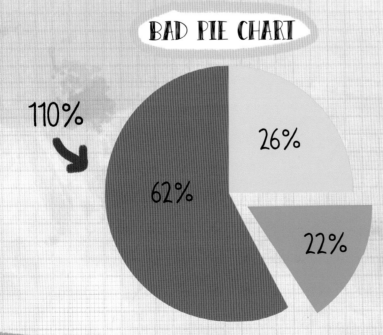

BAD PIE CHART

110%

26%

62%

22%

BOX AND WHISKER PLOT

Statistically this is a very comfortable box!

A box and whisker plot can help you compare different data sets and determine how the data is skewed based on where the median number is within the box.

How do you create a box and whisker plot? Do you get your cat to draw one for you?

If your cat can make one, then you have a pretty cool stat cat! If not, here's what it is and how to make one: a box and whisker plot (which is sometimes called a box plot) is another type of graph that is rather unique. It uses the median of the data set to show you how the data is spread out.

The median is one of five numbers that are used to create a box and whisker plot. It is the middle number of your data set. The other four are the minimum, first quartile, third quartile, and maximum.

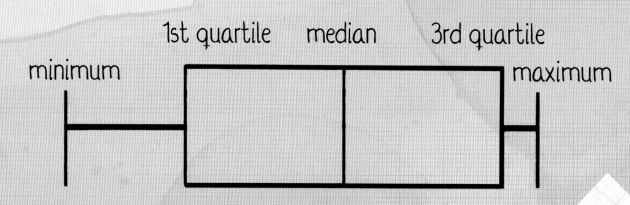

WHAT IS A MEDIAN?

A median is the middle number of the data set. For example, say you have a data set {2, 6, 8, 11, 13, 15, 16}. You would order the numbers from smallest to largest and find the number in the middle. In this case, the median is 11.

To find the maximum and minimum, you would just need to find the largest and the smallest numbers in your data set. For example, if your data set is {2, 6, 8, 11, 13, 15, 16}, then the largest number (maximum) is 16 and the smallest number (minimum) is 2. In this example, 2, 6, and 8 are to the left of the median. That means the first quartile is 6 because it is the median of those three numbers. The third quartile is the median of the numbers to the right of the median: 13, 15, and 16. That means the third quartile is 15. Now you have the 5 number summary, you can graph it!

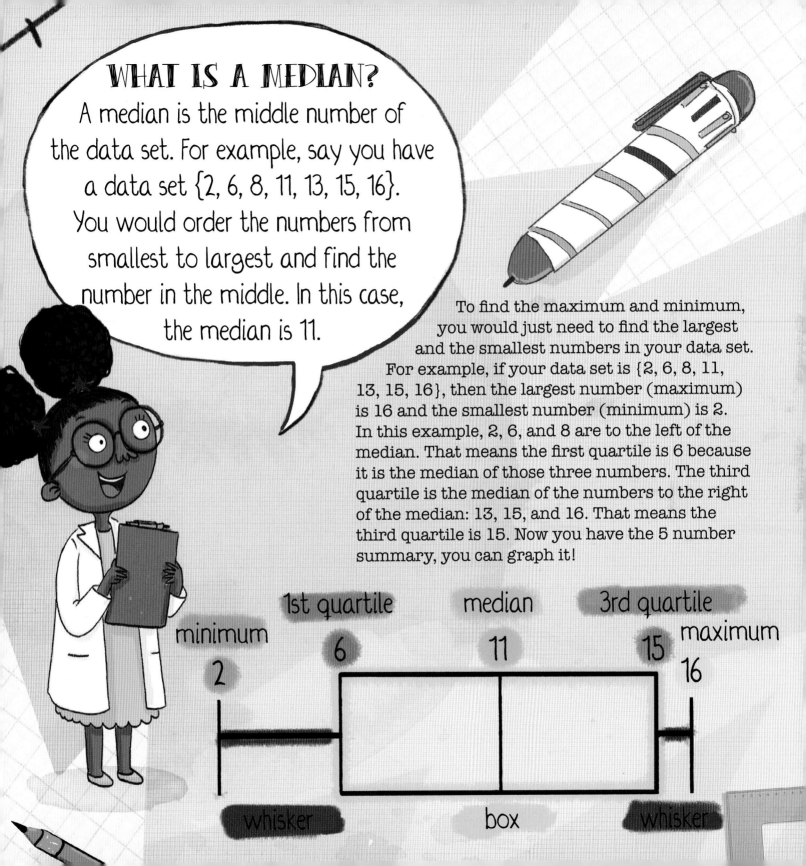

minimum
2

1st quartile
6

median
11

3rd quartile
15

maximum
16

whisker   box   whisker

COLLECTING DATA

Now that you have learned about graphs and data, you are one step closer to being a statistician! The next step is to use data and statistics in your everyday life! Try out some of these activities to use what you have learned about statistics!

Try collecting data and graphing it yourself!

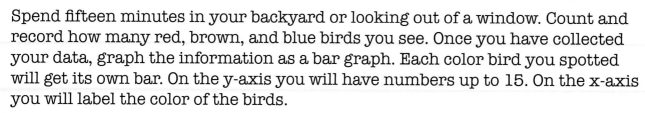

BIRDS

What is the most common bird in your backyard?

Spend fifteen minutes in your backyard or looking out of a window. Count and record how many red, brown, and blue birds you see. Once you have collected your data, graph the information as a bar graph. Each color bird you spotted will get its own bar. On the y-axis you will have numbers up to 15. On the x-axis you will label the color of the birds.

What does your graph tell you? Try it out again at a different time and compare your graphs. Did you notice any changes in your data?

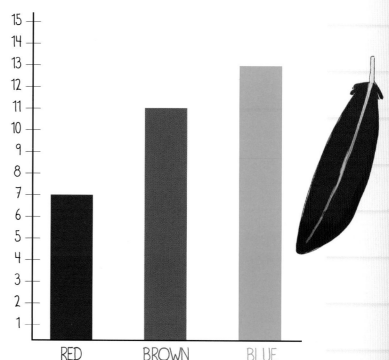

WEATHER

What was the weather like for the week? Were there more sunny days than rainy days?

Track the weather from Monday to Sunday. Record whether it was a sunny day or a cloudy/rainy day. Once you have collected your data, graph the information in a pie chart. If there were 4 days out of 7 days that were sunny, then that is about 57%. You would color a little over 50% of your pie chart to represent the sunny days and the remaining portion would represent the cloudy days.

What does your graph tell you?

Your pie chart won't be exact unless you use tools to help you, but it can give you a pretty good representation of the data you collected.

SUNNY

CLOUDY/ RAINY

Use the prompts below to collect data and create bar graphs and pie charts:

What is your family's favorite ice cream flavor?

What sports do your friends enjoy playing the most?

What do you have for breakfast most often?

How many nights this week did you go to bed before or after 8 pm?

SUIT UP!

Can you beat probability?

●●● ●●●●●

Grab a standard deck of cards and play with a friend or family member!

1. Shuffle the deck thoroughly and then lay the deck on the table face down.

2. Each player takes a turn guessing the suit of the card at the top of the deck.

3. After a guess has been made, the player whose turn it is draws a card.

4. If the player's guess was correct, they get a point.

5. The player who correctly guesses the suit of the top card 10 times wins!

WHAT ARE THE STATS?

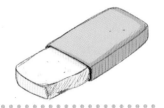

Keep track of points and suits that are drawn on a piece of paper. Once the game is over, draw a bar graph to represent how many times each suit was drawn from the deck.

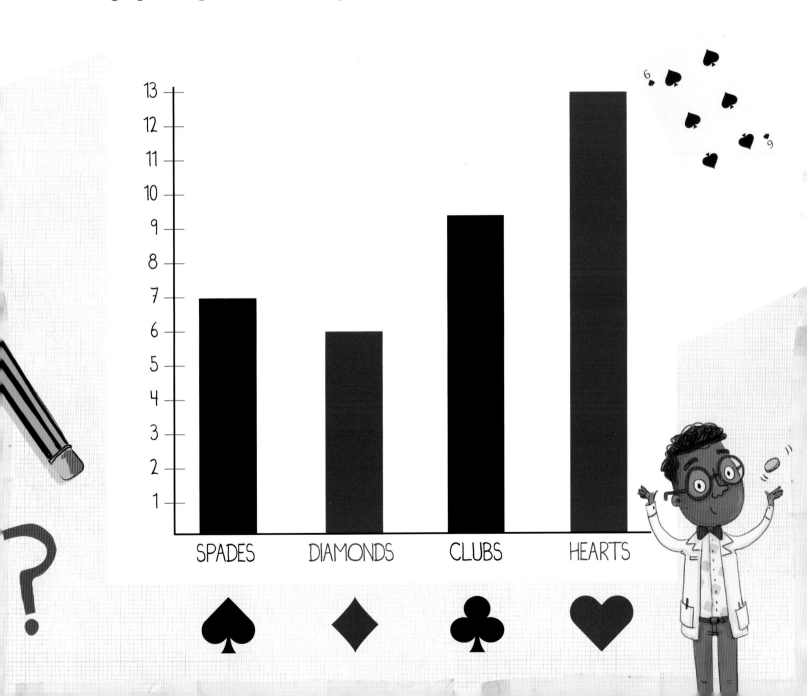

GLOSSARY

Assumption – an idea or opinion you already have about a topic

Bar Graph – a type of graph that uses bars to represent the data; includes two axes (x-axis and y-axis)

Box and Whisker Plot – a type of graph that shows number data and how it is spread out across your population

Clustered Random Sample – a way of representing data in which many different groups represent a larger group

Data – factual information, usually numbers, used in statistics

Data Set – a collection of data

Descriptive Statistics – describes and summarizes data from a specific data set

Hypothesis Testing – conducting a test to see if your hypothesis about a specific population is correct

Inference – an opinion made from known facts or evidence

Inferential Statistics – making an inference about a population based on a smaller sample

Median – the number in the data set that is in the middle

Omitted Variable Bias – a type of bias that happens when one or more relevant variables are not included

Pie Chart – a type of graph in the shape of a circle that represents data as percents in the form of pieces of the circle

Population – the group being used in the test

Recall Bias – a type of bias that happens when the participants omit or misremember details

Simple Random Sample – a sample in which each individual in the population has the opportunity to be chosen

Statistician – an expert in statistics who asks questions and studies groups to answer questions

Statistics – the process of collecting and reviewing data and then presenting your findings

Strata – a select amount of the data that is studied

Stratified Random Sample – data collected from smaller subgroups called strata

Voluntary Response Bias – a type of bias that occurs when the participants are self-selected volunteers